A GUIDE TO T
ARCHAEOLOGY OF I

C000297712

A Guide to the
ARCHAEOLOGY
of
DARTMOOR

DARTMOOR NATIONAL PARK AUTHORITY

First published in Great Britain in 1996 by Devon Books
in association with the Dartmoor National Park Authority

Copyright © 1996 Dartmoor National Park Authority

All rights reserved. No part of this publication may be reproduced,
stored in a retrieval system, or transmitted in any form or by any
means without the prior permission of the copyright holder.

British Library Cataloguing in Publication Data
CIP data for this work is available from the British Library

ISBN 0 86114 904 1

DARTMOOR NATIONAL PARK AUTHORITY
Parke, Bovey Tracey,
Devon TQ13 9JQ
01626 832093

Publishing and sales enquiries to:

DEVON BOOKS
Official Publisher to Devon County Council
Halsgrove House
Lower Moor Way
Tiverton
Devon EX16 6SS
Tel: 01884 243242
Fax: 01884 243325

Printed in Great Britain by Culm Print Ltd., Tiverton

CONTENTS

DATING THE PREHISTORIC AND ROMAN PERIODS

The simplified chronological chart below is intended to provide an approximate dating for the various artefacts and sites recorded in this book.

10,000 BC	8000 BC	4000 BC	2500 BC	1800 BC	1000 BC	700 BC	AD 50
END OF ICE AGE	MESOLITHIC	EARLY — NEOLITHIC — LATE		EARLY — BRONZE AGE — LATE		IRON AGE	ROMAN
FROZEN TUNDRA WITH PRIMITIVE FLORA AND FAUNA. PERMAFROST	BIRCH AND PINE FOREST DEVELOPING. OAK, ELM AND HAZEL WOODLAND IN LOWER AREAS. HEATHER HEATHLAND ON HIGHER AND/OR WETTER AREAS	DENSE OAK FOREST. ELM AND HAZEL GRASSY CLEARANCES AND HEATHER ON UPPER MOOR AND STEEP SLOPES	CLEARANCES FOR AGRICULTURE — ELM DECLINE.	OPEN GRASSLAND WITH REMNANT OAK FOREST IN VALLEY BOTTOMS	CLIMATIC DETERIORATION		DEVELOPING HEATHLAND WITH REMNANT OAK FOREST
	ARTIFICIAL CLEARANCES TO ATTRACT GAME	— CEREALS —					
UNINHABITED	HUNTERS AND GATHERERS	FIRST FARMERS – MIXED ECONOMY —	FARMERS PREDOMINANTLY STOCK RAISING —				
	STONE AND FLINT TOOLS FROM THE MOOR	STONE AND FLINT TOOLS FOUND ON THE MOOR					
		CHAMBERED TOMBS					
			IRREGULAR FIELD SYSTEMS				
			REGULAR AND EXTENSIVE FIELD SYSTEMS (REAVES)				
			STONE CIRCLES				
			STONE ROWS AND STANDING STONES				
			ROUND CAIRNS AND CISTS				
			HUT CIRCLES				
			ENCLOSURES				
			HILL FORTS				

Based on information prepared by Dr. Alex Gibson (1988)

INTRODUCTION

This is a guide to the archaeology of Dartmoor. The word 'archaeology', in its purest sense, means the *study* of the material remains of our past, although we now commonly use the term to refer to the visible remains in the landscape. The archaeology of any area illustrates the way in which people have responded to the local environment – to the geology and vegetation which have given them building materials, and the minerals which have contributed to the local economy; to the fertility of the soils and the climate which have dictated the way in which the landscape has been farmed; and to the topography which has influenced where settlements are sited and where communications have been established.

The archaeology of Dartmoor is very special. Within today's wild moorland landscapes, dominated by heather and moorland grasses, can be found extensive remains of past human activity – much now reclaimed by nature. Here can be seen prehistoric ritual and burial sites, some dating as far back as the fourth millennium BC, field systems and settlements three and a half thousand years old; medieval farmsteads and associated fields established nearly ten centuries ago; and remains of a tin industry which is certainly 700 years old and possibly much older, and which only ceased during the early years of this century. Other, more recent industrial activity is also recorded in the landscape.

The exceptionally good survival of Dartmoor's visible archaeological remains is largely due to the durability of the local granite used for building, and to the limited extent of modern exploitation and intensive agricultural development on the moor. Much of Dartmoor's archaeology is now recognised as being of national and international importance.

Dartmoor offers a chance not just to view a collection of individual and isolated monuments left over from the past but also a rare opportunity to discover complete and integrated *landscapes* that illustrate the way in which people have lived, worked and died for more than 6,000 years. Where else, for example, can be found over 10,000ha. (25,000 acres) of prehistoric fields, and associated dwellings?

Dartmoor has often been described as an archaeological *palimpsest* – meaning that it is possible to read the landscape like a book with transparent pages, so that the remains of each period of occupation are visible through those of later times. Any tract of land on the moor might well contain a variety monuments dating from 4000 BC to the present century. These landscapes and their monuments are important sources of information about our history, and provide a tangible link with our distant and not so distant past.

The individual monuments and features which make up these complex and rich landscapes are numerous. This booklet is an introduction to many of the earthworks and stone structures which any visitor might encounter, but it is not comprehensive; such a work would be many times longer than this. Standing buildings (and their ruined counterparts) are not, by and large, included.

The booklet is divided into four sections – prehistory, medieval, industry, and byways and boundaries. The first three sections begin with a general description of the relevant period, offering a context for the visible archaeological remains. These are followed by illustrated glossaries of the main types of monuments which may be seen. Those monuments described in the general section which appear in the glossaries are given in capital letters in colour the first time they appear. Although reference is sometimes made to the artefacts (objects) made and used in the past, these have not been illustrated. A brief explanation of the terms used to describe the different prehistoric periods appears on page 6.

Individual sites are only mentioned, exceptionally, where it is necessary to illustrate a particular point in the text. This is not a guide to sites of interest, for these extend into many thousands, and there is no gazetteer. The purpose of this booklet is help you to recognise the different types of monument that are on Dartmoor.

There are probably as many as 10,000 individual archaeological monuments on Dartmoor; many of these are protected by law (the *Ancient Monuments and Archaeological Areas Act, 1979*), and it is a criminal offence to damage or interfere with them in any way. You should be aware that some sites particularly those associated with past mineral working, can be dangerous.

Some technical terms are used in the text. Most are explained in the glossaries. Frequent use is made of the term millennium – a period of 1,000 years; thus the second millennium BC represents the period between 2,000 and 1,000 years before the Birth of Christ (BC) and the first millennium AD represents the first 1,000 years after that event (Anno Domini).

KEY

Key words which appear in the text in green type refer to specific illustrations in the glossary. The symbols below are repeated at the top of each page and provide easy referencing between the main text section and the relevant glossary pages.

 PREHISTORIC DARTMOOR

 MEDIEVAL DARTMOOR

 INDUSTRIAL DARTMOOR

 BOUNDARIES AND BYWAYS

PREHISTORIC DARTMOOR

The terms mesolithic, neolithic, Bronze Age and Iron Age have been used in this booklet. These are the conventional terms used to divide up the long period known as prehistory, and chart technological development. The mesolithic (or middle Stone Age) identifies a period between about 8000 and 4000 BC, when tiny flint tools were produced. The neolithic period (or new Stone Age: c.4000-2500 BC) saw the introduction of different types of stone tools, the domestication of plants and animals, and the construction of large megalithic monuments. During the Bronze Age (c.2500–600 BC), metal working began and a rich array of archaeological sites and features, both ritual and secular, survive from the period. In the Iron Age (c.600 BC–AD 43), as the name suggests, the development of iron-smelting occurs, and the creation of large defended settlements known as hillforts.

However, we are becoming increasingly aware that these terms are an over-simplification and that change was much more gradual and less easily defined than was once thought. Nevertheless, since most people are familiar with these nomenclatures, they have been used in this booklet.

EARLY VISITORS
8000 – 4000 BC
The Mesolithic Period

By 10,000 BC, the last ice-sheets had receded and the climate became warmer. This resulted in tundra-like vegetation of southern England changing to a landscape of trees. Studies of buried ancient pollens from Dartmoor show that by 8000 BC it had a mainly oak woodland cover along its river valleys and lower slopes, giving way to mixed deciduous trees (predominantly hazel and birch) on higher ground; whilst the highest areas were open moorland containing a few isolated trees.

The large animals that had grazed the tundra grasslands were replaced fairly rapidly by the woodland species of deer, wild oxen and pig. This change had an important consequence for the hunting and gathering lifestyle of the prehistoric people living in the area. The woodland animals were less gregarious than the great herds which had lived on the tundra plains, and the woodland environment supported fewer mammals – thus the food supply was reduced, and hunting became more difficult. It is probable that at this time Dartmoor would have been used as a seasonal source of food (not only of meat but also of nuts and berries), with mesolithic peoples moving between the inland and coastal areas of Devon during the year.

Pollen and peat studies on Dartmoor have shown that throughout the mesolithic period, particularly between about 5500 and 4300 BC, small clearances in the woodland cover were created, some as a result of fire; the inference is that this was the work of humans. Wild animals would have been drawn into the clearings in the woodland cover to graze, and once there, could be killed with relative ease. The combination of burning and grazing began the slow spread of the blanket peat bog which now covers so much of the high moor. In this way, the conversion of a forest to today's open landscape began.

Evidence for the presence of mesolithic people on Dartmoor lies in the scatters of small tools fashioned from flint known as *microliths*, which have been found in areas of disturbed ground. The microliths often occur near springs and could represent the sites of temporary hunting camps.

MONUMENTS OF THE FIRST FARMERS
4000 – 2500 BC
The Neolithic Period

The neolithic period in Britain witnessed a gradual change from a wandering lifestyle to a more settled one, as both animals and crops were domesticated and the deliberate cultivation of food plants was introduced.

On Dartmoor, as in other upland areas, hunting remained important, and here the impact of farming on the landscape does not appear to have been dramatic. Pollen evidence from various locations has indicated some clearance of larger trees and their replacement by herbs, grasses and weeds of cultivation. Timber was felled using heavily polished or finely chipped stone axeheads. Flint was still being worked; the microliths were replaced by larger knives, blades and scrapers. The leaf-shaped arrowheads of flint of this period which have been found on the moor are evidence for the continued importance of hunting at this time.

It is from this period that the earliest visible structures survive – the CHAMBER TOMBS These are stone-built chambers within which multiple burials were placed, and which were sited at one end of long earth and stone mounds. Their construction must have required the co-ordinated labour of a cohesive community, and they may well have also served as landscape markers, defining sizeable territories. Their dilapidated appearance today does not adequately reflect their former significance.

During the fourth millennium BC, in other parts of the south-west, tribal centres developed, perhaps controlling relatively large territories. Two such sites have been tentatively identified on Dartmoor – at Dewerstone Rock and White Tor, where low stone walls encircle the tors.

CEREMONY AND RITUAL
c 2500 – 1500 BC
The Later Neolithic to Early/Middle Bronze Age

The introduction of metalworking and its influence upon prehistoric societies was more gradual than immediate, and the ceremonial monuments of Dartmoor straddle the conventional division between the later neolithic and Bronze Age periods. Lack of modern excavation and research precludes too precise a dating of many of the monuments which characterise this period. However, it is clear that at this time a wide range and number of monuments associated with burial and ritual were being constructed on Dartmoor.

To what degree the moor was being used for other purposes is unclear; its wild animal population continued to offer a valuable resource to the hunter. At the same time, continued clearance of the forest cover in the higher regions would have provided summer grazing for domesticated animals living at lower levels. It is also thought that these clearings might have been used occasionally for arable cultivation.

Burial practices underwent a change. The chamber tombs, with their long earthen mounds were replaced by ROUND CAIRNS of varying size. Some of the larger examples (such as Giant's Basin at Drizzlecombe) may be of early (ie late neolithic) date. Others, sometimes known as 'prestige' cairns, may belong to the end of this period. These latter cairns are often sited in a prominent position, on ridges or on hilltops, and may have fulfilled twin roles – serving as burials and territorial markers. The larger cairns may at first have covered a single burial, but it is thought that they, and the area around them, may have been used thereafter for the burial of other members of the family or community.

The smaller round cairns of this period probably mark the site of a single burial. A number of these small mounds cover a CIST (pronounced *kist*), a stone box sunk into the ground, into which a body or cremated ashes were placed. A number of cists can be found in association with stone rows (see page 30). Some cist burials are surrounded by CAIRN CIRCLES or KERB CIRCLES which define the area of the monument.

A few examples of MULTIPLE STONE CIRCLES have been found on Dartmoor. Here, concentric rings of upright stones can be seen poking up through cairn material.

These burial cairns are assumed to have belonged to the aristocracy, that is, to those individuals who were most highly regarded by their communities. The acidic nature of Dartmoor's soils has destroyed organic material, such as bone, and no trace of the burial itself survives. In some examples, minor grave goods have been discovered. These include fragments of decorated beaker-shaped pottery and barbed and tanged flint arrowheads, both of which may have come into the area at the same time as metalworking.

Not all types of cairn can be directly associated with burial. The only examples of a RING CAIRN (where a flat area is defined by a roughly circular, stone rubble bank) excavated on Dartmoor revealed no evidence for burial, but are thought to have served some sort of cenotaphic function. Some of Dartmoor's tors and naturally occurring outcrops of granite were ringed by low, stone banks or partially covered by round cairns; these are known as TOR CAIRNS. Groups of up to 30 or so small cairns, known as CAIRNFIELDS, can be found particularly in the north west part of the moor. Some of these may cover burials, others may be CLEARANCE CAIRNS associated with agricultural practices.

Round cairns and cist burials can sometimes be found at the end of lines of upright stones or STONE ROWS. A greater concentration of stone rows can be found on Dartmoor than anywhere else in Britain, but their purpose remains an enigma. Stone rows seem to have been constructed within clearings in the forest cover. Their association with burial monuments would indicate that they had a religious or ritual significance. It has also been argued that some at least, of the stone rows are aligned towards astronomical features or occurrences, such as the position of the sun or moon at one of the solstices. They might, therefore, represent a fusion of the spiritual and the practical. Stone rows may have been used as seasonal sun dials, marking the passing of winter into spring and significant events in the agricultural calendar. To primitive societies whose way of life was governed by the seasons, it would not be surprising if these features took on a mystical or religious importance. They may also have been territorial centres or boundaries. In more recent times, the parish church has provided just such a complex function – as a religious, social, community and geographical centre.

As with the burial monuments of Dartmoor, there is considerable variety in the architecture of its stone rows. There are both single and double (parallel) rows and even more complex alignments of set stones. The stones themselves vary between the tall and the short; and the terminal features can include burials, blocking stones and menhirs.

The MENHIR, a distinctively tall, upright stone, can also be found both near to but detached from other ceremonial monuments, and in complete isolation. We assume that, like the stone rows, the menhir served both ritual and practical functions.

Free-standing STONE CIRCLES, enclosing an area without any apparent burial, can also be found on Dartmoor, sometimes near stone rows. Their purpose, although probably ceremonial, remains unclear.

THE FARMED LANDSCAPE
c 1700 – 600 BC
The Bronze Age

The middle of the second millennium BC was to see the most intensive use of Dartmoor as a controlled, settled and farmed landscape. Much of the high moor which now offers rather poor grazing for livestock, had less acidic soils during the middle Bronze Age, and was valuable pasture land. The widespread clearance of much of the remaining tree cover at this time, together with intensive grazing, accelerated the formation of peat.

The Bronze Age is the earliest period on Dartmoor from which the remains of houses and allied structures survive. HUT CIRCLES – of which perhaps more

14

than 3,000 examples survive today – were the standard building form. Many were constructed of drystone granite walls and would have had conical timber and thatched roofs. Some may have been shelters for shepherds; others may have been more permanent dwellings; yet others may have been used for the storage of cereals, housing of animals or as weaving sheds and so on. It is important to remember that what we see today are the remains of buildings which, when fully equipped and in use, would have been much more spacious and comfortable than their present derelict appearance would suggest.

Recent archaeological excavations have found that many of the stone-built huts had timber predecessors which have left no trace above ground, and that even the remains of stone buildings visible today may have had contemporary timber structures nearby.

Many hut circles are located near river valleys, which were heavily worked for tin ore in medieval times. As both tin and copper (the constituent ingredients for bronze) are to be found on Dartmoor and in the surrounding area, it is not unreasonable to assume that prehistoric people were using these mineral resources. A number of bronze artefacts (axes and palstaves, for example) have been found on the edge of the moor, where the less acidic soils have allowed their preservation.

Hut circles can be found in isolation, in clusters (known as open settlements), within walled ENCLOSURES (often called pounds) and within field systems, sometimes attached to the field walls. Near Rippon Tor (not far from Widecombe-in-the-Moor), a single hut stands against a perimeter wall enclosing three square fields, with a yard in front of the house. Homesteads like this are features of the eastern side of the moor. The clusters of hut circles are mostly concentrated on the western side of Dartmoor in the upper river valleys. Enclosed groups occur chiefly in the southern river valleys. Excavation of an enclosure at Shaugh Moor on the south western edge of the moor revealed that the enclosure wall was added some three centuries after the construction of the first hut circle. There was no entrance in the wall, but there were footings for a stile, suggesting that the wall was built to keep stock away from the living area. At Grimspound (eastern Dartmoor), on the other hand, the enclosure wall is substantial and has an imposing gateway, which may indicate a more defensive character.

Our knowledge of the detail of prehistoric animal husbandry is handicapped by the fact that no bones have survived. However, due to a rare circumstance in the past, the footprints of animals alive on Shaugh Moor some three and a half thousand years ago were preserved. During the excavations of a pre-historic field boundary, the footprints of sheep, cattle, ponies and even a badger were discovered in buried soil in the ditch which ran alongside it. In the nearby enclosure were found spindle whorls – used in spinning – and fragments of quern stones on which grain was ground into flour. These show that cereal crops were being grown, but the analysis of ancient pollen indicates that arable farming played a secondary role, and the predominant use of the moor at this time was for the pasturing of animals. Radio-carbon dating from the Shaugh Moor enclosure shows that the settlement was in use for well over half a millenium (from about 1700 BC to 1200 or 1000 BC). The small number of objects recovered during the excavation as well as the lack of hearths in the hut circles, suggested that this was a seasonal settlement, used by people and animals who spent the winter months at sites on the lower contours. Other settlements, however, may well have been occupied throughout the year.

It is clear that a sense of ownership of land became increasingly important from the middle of the second millennium BC. This has been shown by recent archaeological work on the REAVES, perhaps the most characteristic features of the prehistoric landscape of Dartmoor, dating from around 1500 BC. Reaves (the local name given to prehistoric land boundaries) are now visible as low, stony, earth covered banks. They cover an extensive part of the open moor, although they are notably absent from the north western quarter. Over 200km (125 miles) of reaves have been identified, enclosing over 10,000ha (25,000 acres) of land. They also extended into what are still enclosed landscapes on the fringes of the moor, and many field boundaries in use today have their origins some three and a half thousand years ago.

The reaves offer evidence for a highly organised system of land division, initiated during the middle centuries of the second millennium BC. The lower slopes of Dartmoor were divided from the higher areas by terminal reaves, which ran along the contours. The lower areas were subdivided by parallel reaves running at right angles to the terminal reaves, and the long narrow strips thus created were themselves subdivided by cross reaves. In some areas, especially in the south and west, more irregular boundaries known as contour reaves can be found above the terminal reaves. Thus the landscape seems to have been zoned into three divisions – firstly, the most intensively used areas represented by the parallel reave systems; secondly, an inter-mediate area between these and the contour reaves; and thirdly, above these, the highest, unenclosed land. We can speculate that these zones reflect the way in which the land was used for grazing; the better pastures on the lower areas required more control of stock than those on the higher areas, which may have been used for extensive (as opposed to intensive) and perhaps seasonal grazing, much as the commons of Dartmoor were used during the medieval period.

From about 1000 BC the climate deteriorated. Cooler summers and wetter conditions, together with the formation of blanket peat which produced impoverished vegetation, meant that it became increasingly more difficult to sustain earlier levels of grazing and cereal growing. This probably contributed to a slow abandonment of sites – a retreat to the lower and more easily farmed areas.

THE END OF THE PREHISTORIC PERIOD
600 BC – AD 43
The Iron Age

The final centuries of the prehistoric era saw the gradual introduction and adoption of iron for the manufacture of tools and weapons. The transition between the Bronze Age and the Iron Age was, like that between the neolithic and the Bronze Age much more gradual than the abrupt change of name implies, and the introduction of iron-working brought about no immediate change. The gradual abandonment of the higher moor continued during this period. Evidence for Iron Age occupation of hut circles has been revealed in excavations carried out at settlements which lie on the extreme edge of the open moor. Radio-carbon dates and pottery from one site (Gold Park, near Grimspound) suggest occupation to the very end of the first millennium BC; in one of the huts at Kestor, near Chagford, evidence of iron-working was found.

The later Iron Age saw the appearance of a new type of site – the HILLFORT; about twelve are to be found on the fringes of the open moor. These hilltop settlements of hut circles were heavily defended by ramparts and ditches; they are indications of a society which was becoming increasingly tribal and aggressive in nature. They were probably focal points within large territories, used as market centres and/or areas of retreat.

MEDIEVAL DARTMOOR

Although we know that the fringes of the moor were settled in the later pre-historic period (Iron Age), it is not clear from the evidence so far available, how long this occupation continued. The four centuries of the Roman military occupation of Britain (c. AD 43–410) are not represented in the archaeology of Dartmoor; the nearest evidence for Roman military presence in the first century AD lies in a temporary fort established just north of Okehampton.

There are signs of human activity around Dartmoor in the immediate post-Roman period, sometimes called the Dark Ages. Inscribed POST-ROMAN MEMORIAL STONES, commemorating tribal leaders or princes of the 5th–7th centuries have been found on the edges of the high moor, particularly on the north and west sides. Parish churches dedicated to Celtic missionaries from Ireland and Wales suggest Dark Age settlement; St Petroc, a Welsh missionary of the 5th century, is commemorated at Lydford, South Brent and Harford.

The evidence is too slight for us to be able to reconstruct the Dartmoor of this period, although it does suggest that activity was confined to the moorland fringes. Study of buried pollen on the Moor to the south of Okehampton, indicates that there at least, the open pasture of the prehistoric period was reverting to scrub and woodland, suggesting that the open moor was being little used to graze stock.

A slight improvement in the climate in the latter part of the first millennium AD (the centuries preceding the Norman Conquest) brought about an increase in population, and the resulting need to provide more food pushed farming communities back on to the deserted moor. By this time, Dartmoor was, in agricultural terms, marginal land providing relatively poor pasture and low crop yields. From this period onwards it witnessed an ebb and flow of occupation; land was taken in and farmed during periods of high population, economic security and favourable weather, and abandoned when these trends were reversed.

From at least the 10th century, areas of Dartmoor which had not been farmed since prehistoric times were recolonised – principally the lower contours of the high moor and the hinterlands of the major rivers. Much of central Dartmoor became a Royal Forest – land reserved for the Kings of England, and later the Earls and Dukes of Cornwall, to hunt deer and other wild beasts. Nevertheless, there were certain rights of pasture granted to farmers around the moor (and indeed throughout Devon) and a number of farms, known as Ancient Tenements, were permitted to be founded within the Forest.

Typically, the medieval farmer on Dartmoor lived in a LONGHOUSE, in which people and animals were sheltered under a common roof, animals at one end, people at the other. The earliest surviving examples are of the 13th century, with walls of roughly-coursed granite.

Remains of these longhouses are found either isolated or grouped together in hamlets. Small dwellings, outhouses and CORN-DRYING BARNS can sometimes be seen in association with longhouses and also small gardens.

It is generally assumed that the animal part of the longhouse was occupied by cattle, including perhaps oxen which were used to draw the plough (see page 39). Sheep were an important element of husbandry in the medieval period on Dartmoor. Animal bones do not survive in Dartmoor's acidic soils, so we lack archaeological evidence for other stock. However, the Domesday Book (1086) records the presence of pigs and goats on a number of Dartmoor manors.

Evidence from charred grains discovered in excavation and from buried pollen samples indicates that cereal crops were being grown – oats, barley and rye, and to a lesser extent wheat. Often, land put down to cultivation was shared between neighbouring farmers, each taking a number of small, elongated strips of about half a hectare (1 acre) each, scattered throughout the large fields lying closest to the settlement sites – called INFIELDS; beyond these lay the OUTFIELDS, used for the most part for grazing stock, but which were ploughed and sown with cereals when necessary. The boundary between the farmed land and the open moor, formed by common land and the Forest of Dartmoor, was marked by CORN-DITCHES

This practice of sharing cultivated land (probably as a means of ensuring equal distribution of good and bad soils amongst the community) led to the creation, on sloping land, of terraces known as STRIP LYNCHETS Another common result of medieval and later cultivation is RIDGE AND FURROW, probably created to produce deeper soils and better drainage. During the later medieval and subsequent periods, the practice of sharing land died out – although not everywhere at the same time – and strips were enclosed (ENCLOSED STRIPS) by hedgebanks, either individually or grouped together in parcels, and worked as a single unit.

A number of the farms that were created on the margins of Dartmoor in the early medieval period were abandoned towards the end of the 14th century/beginning of the 15th century. From AD 1300 or so, the climate had been growing steadily worse. Animals were probably suffering through poor grazing and disease engendered by cold and wet conditions, and crops could no longer ripen naturally in the fields. The Black Death swept through Devon in the 1340s and reduced its population by possibly as much as two-thirds. This enabled some of the Dartmoor farmers to move away from areas from where it was difficult to eke out a living. Many of the settlements which were deserted at this time lie just above the present-day boundary between enclosed land and the moor.

These deserted sites do not by any means suggest a total abandonment of Dartmoor, and indeed in the centuries which followed, the area enjoyed a period of prosperity which owed much to both sheep husbandry and tin working.

Wool was an important source of wealth in the later medieval period. A significant amount of land on Dartmoor was owned by the monasteries of Buckland, Buckfast and Tavistock, which contributed to and shared in the prosperity enjoyed by Devon in a woollen industry famed throughout Europe. Archaeological evidence as such for sheep is rather poor, and we have to rely on documentary sources – the records of the monasteries, markets and ports, references to fulling mills (where wool was processed), and so on – to testify to their importance.

The rabbit too played a part in Dartmoor's economy; from the medieval period it was exploited for food and fur. Artificial buries or PILLOW MOUNDS were constructed to provide attractive accommodation, and the rabbits were protected from predators by VERMIN TRAPS.

The abandoned medieval sites on Dartmoor exemplify the basic settlement pattern of the area – farmsteads are either found in isolation or clustered together in hamlets. Imposed upon this arrangement (which echoes that of the prehistoric period) are the villages and towns of the Moor. Little study of their origins has been made; nevertheless it is probable that most of these nucleated settlements grew up in the later medieval period (ie after the time of the Norman Conquest). They served as locations of fairs and of markets for the distribution and exchange of goods. The prosperity of three moorland towns – Ashburton, Chagford and Tavistock – was enhanced by their designation in the 13th century as Stannary Towns, for the assaying of tin. Only two settlements have identifiable and datable origins: Lydford was established in the late 9th or early 10th century AD by the kings of Wessex as a *burh* – a settlement defended against possible Viking attack. The Saxon ramparts enclosing the promontory upon which the town was sited can still be seen. The main street and the lanes leading from it at right angles form one of our earliest examples of town planning. South Zeal, on the northern fringes of Dartmoor, was founded in 1299 by the Lord of the Manor of South Tawton, in what proved to be an unsuccessful attempt to create a new market centre. Here can be seen the topography of a typical medieval town – houses along the street frontage, with long narrow BURGAGE PLOTS extending back from them. Vestiges of similar burgage plots can be found in other Dartmoor towns.

The classic monuments of medieval times are 'CASTLES, monasteries and CHURCHES. Three medieval castles can be seen on Dartmoor – a Norman ringwork at Lydford, and motte and bailey castles at Okehampton and Hembury, near Buckfastleigh. The three great abbeys of the medieval period were established on the fringes of Dartmoor – at Tavistock (in 981), Buckfast (1018) and Buckland (1278). All have undergone considerable change since the Reformation in the 16th century, and comparatively little medieval fabric can be seen easily. Church architecture reflects the period of a community's greatest wealth, and on Dartmoor this was to be found in the 15th and 16th centuries, when profits from the wool and tin industries made possible the refurbishment and enlargement of earlier structures. Most of Dartmoor's churches thus exhibit architecture of the style known as Perpendicular.

INDUSTRIAL
DARTMOOR

Although now very much a rural landscape, regarded by many as an area of natural wilderness, Dartmoor has in the past witnessed much industrial activity. In particular, it has been a major producer of tin, but also of other minerals such as copper. The industries of Dartmoor are many and varied – mining, quarrying, lime-burning, even arsenic production, gun-powder manufacture and ice-making. This chapter does not attempt to describe all the complexities of Dartmoor's industrial archaeology but looks only at its most typical and accessible features.

The archaeological landscape of Dartmoor is dominated by the remains of the tin industry. There are good reasons for supposing that the rich veins of cassiterite (tin ore) found within the granite mass were exploited by pre-historic peoples although at present archaeological evidence for this is weak. Tin together with copper, which can be found on the periphery of the moor, combine to form bronze, the alloy that gives its name to one of the major periods of prehistory. However, it is the work of the medieval and later tin-miners that has left an enduring impression upon the face of Dartmoor. Tin is not only a major component of bronze but also (with lead) of pewter.

The industry reached its peak in the 16th century AD, but had been important from at least the 12th century (from which time the first documentary record survives). A revival occurred during the late 18th century, and activity did not finally cease until 1930.

Deposits of tin ore are confined in England to Dartmoor and parts of Cornwall; this scarcity rendered it a valuable commodity. In the medieval and post-medieval periods the industry was controlled by the Crown, for whom it was an important source of revenue. In 1201, a charter of King John confirmed the ancient rights of the tinners '...to mine for tine and dig turves for smelting tin, anywhere in our lands, moors and wastes...'. Despite some records of conflict between the apparently opposing interests of tin-working and agriculture, on the whole the two activities seem to have taken place in some degree of harmony; it is thought that tenant farmers may themselves have been part-time tinners or to have held shares in workings on their land.

Dartmoor was divided into four areas known as *Stannaries* (a word deriving from the Latin *stannum*, meaning tin). Tinners were required to bring their ingots four times a year to one of four Stannary Towns (Ashburton, Chagford, Tavistock, created in 1305, or Plympton, created in 1328). Here the ingots were weighed, tested for purity (assayed or *coigned*) and a tax levied upon them. The industry was governed by its own customs and laws, under the jurisdiction of the Lord Warden of the Stannaries and courts were set up to settle differences and right wrongs. A Stannary courthouse and gaol was built at Lydford in the late 12th century, now known somewhat erroneously as Lydford Castle. The last of the Stannary courts is believed to have been held in 1786, and they were formally abolished in 1836. Between 1494 and 1749, 11 Great Courts, or Tinners' Parliaments, are known to have been held at Crockern Tor in the heart of Dartmoor. Here jurates from the four Stannaries met to agree regulations and statutes for the industry.

As well as providing revenue for the Crown, Dartmoor tin brought prosperity to the local population, and funded the rebuilding of many parish churches during the 15th and 16th centuries and the construction of a number of fine houses.

The revival of the tin industry on Dartmoor in the 18th and 19th centuries coincided with technological advances, increased demand for metals created by the Industrial Revolution and the development of tin-plating. There were probably some 50 or so mines operating on Dartmoor during this period. Companies were set up under such names as 'The Devon Great Tincroft Tin-mining Company' and 'Dartmoor United Tin Mines'.

Many companies only seem to have lasted a few years before mines were abandoned or restarted under new management. In some of the larger mines, up to 100 people were employed, including women and children. Often the miners travelled long distances from their homes to work, and lived for the better part of the week in dormitories near the workings. The industry declined during the latter part of the 19th century and, despite some activity in the 1920s and 30s, had effectively come to an end after the First World War.

The medieval tinners worked the alluvial deposits of cassiterite, extracting the tin-bearing stones from the beds of streams and rivers, agitating the water so that the lighter waste materials would be washed away. Areas of STREAM-WORKING are characterised by spoil heaps of small stones in the valley bottoms. Often the spoil is arranged in straight or curving parallel ridges, which were used to divert the water from its original course on to fresh deposits of alluvial tin.

In later times, by the 15th century at least, tin lodes below the ground surface were being exploited. Prospecting for tin resulted in the excavation of TRIAL PITS along the lines of suspected lodes. Where tin ore was discovered, it was mined either by the excavation of a line of LODE-BACK PITS or deep V-shaped gullies, known as 'beams' or OPENWORKS; most date from the period before 1700. Shallow shafts were sometimes sunk at the bottom of the openworks.

Although SHAFT-MINING was practised from the 16th century, most of the mine shafts visible on Dartmoor belong to the late 18th and 19th centuries. Associated with these are the horizontal ADITS, drainage or access tunnels.

In order to extract pure tin from its parent rock, the ore had first to be crushed and concentrated. After this, it was smelted and turned into ingots. Although crushing ('knocking' or 'stamping' as it is known) and smelting ('blowing') were sometimes carried out on separate sites, before about 1750 they often combined in a single building, or TIN MILL. The processes were powered by water, which was brought to a wheel adjacent to the mill building via an artificial channel, or LEAT. The ore was placed upon granite MORTAR STONES inside the mill, where it was crushed by STAMPS, powered by the waterwheel. The crushed ore was concentrated nearby in DRESSING FLOORS and BUDDLES, shallow depressions in which water was used to wash away waste material and separate heavier, richer ores from the lighter ones. The waterwheel also operated a set of bellows within the mill, which raised the temperature inside the FURNACE, where the crushed ore was smelted. The molten ore was then poured into a MOULDSTONE. The rights granted of old to tinners to dig turves, allowed them to use the Dartmoor peat for fuel in the furnaces. Wood charcoal was also used, and many of Dartmoor's woodlands contain CHARCOAL BURNERS' HEARTHS.

Remains of late 18th-, 19th- and early 20th-century tin processing areas include stamping mills (where the ore was crushed), and more sophisticated examples of buddles and dressing floors. By this time, smelting had largely ceased to take place on Dartmoor. Unlike Cornwall, where the engine house dominates the industrial landscape, water remained the principal source of power on Dartmoor. Often very large WHEELPITS can be found close to mine shafts; the waterwheels were used to pump water from underground.

Structures associated with the tin industry can also sometimes be found –

tinners' shelters and BEEHIVE HUTS, which were probably used as stores. The modern mines also contain the remains of a variety of buildings – accommodation for miners and the mine captains' offices, blacksmiths' and carpenters' workshops and DRYS, where the miners could dry out their clothing, and themselves!

Although tin was the pre-eminent industry, other natural resources of Dartmoor have been exploited in the past. The 'metamorphic aureole' around the edge of the granite mass contains a variety of minerals which have been worked – most extensively in the last couple of centuries. These include copper, silver, lead and iron. By the mid-19th century, a significant amount of the world supply of copper came from four mines in and around Dartmoor; the remains of the mines at Wheal Friendship, near Mary Tavy cover more than 12ha (30 acres). The industry fell into decline towards the close of the century. Micaceous haematite, a shiny iron ore, used mainly in the production of rust-resisting paints, was mined in the area of Bovey Tracey until the 1960s.

In many ways the remains of these industries are similar to those associated with the winning and working of tin – shafts, spoil heaps, wheelpits, leats and workshops. Some of the very few examples of the ENGINE HOUSE to be found on Dartmoor, however, occur at the copper, silver and lead mines around its periphery.

Granite has been the predominant building stone since prehistoric times, but was not quarried until the 19th century. Before then, the stone (moorstone) was taken from the surface. It was used unworked in prehistoric times, and occasionally 'dressed' and/or carved by medieval stonemasons. Before about 1800, granite was cut using the WEDGE AND GROOVE method; after 1800 the stone was split by a method known as FEATHER AND TARE. Dartmoor is full of granite artefacts e.g. GATEPOSTS, TROUGHS, CRUSHES and PRESSES, MILL-STONES; some still in their original positions in fields or farmsteads, others now adorning patios and back gardens. Many of these artefacts were manufactured on site, out on the open moor, to minimise the cost and labour of moving heavy stone. SETT-MAKERS' BANKERS can occasionally be discovered – crude stone benches used by masons in the preparation of paving stones, kerbs and setts. So also can be seen a few examples of artefacts where something went wrong during manufacture and which were therefore abandoned.

The first granite quarries were opened at the end of the 18th century, and the industry expanded with the arrival of the railways. Granite from the

Dartmoor quarries was used in the construction of London Bridge and the British Museum, to name but two examples.

The Dartmoor peat has been exploited as a source of fuel for generations, for both domestic and commercial reasons. Peat cuttings are best appreciated from the air – from where the long, rectangular strips of the cuttings are easily visible. On the ground they form uneven surfaces.

The CHINA CLAY industry, which in its modern form dominates the landscape of south-west Dartmoor, began more than 150 years ago, and the earliest remains now form another part of Dartmoor's industrial heritage.

Many of Dartmoor's industries in the 19th century were served by TRAMWAYS or railways. Before the advent of the iron railroad, horse-drawn carts were pulled along granite setts, the best surviving example of which can be seen on Haytor Down.

BOUNDARIES
AND BYWAYS

COMMUNICATIONS

Getting from one part of Dartmoor to another has never been easy. The moor
is traversed by rivers and streams, difficult to cross, endowed with treacher-
ous bogs and in places lacks easily recognisable landmarks. CLAPPER
BRIDGES were first constructed in medieval times and the last known
example was built in the latter part of the 19th century. Many of the granite
CROSSES which are so much a part of the Dartmoor landscape were probably
erected in the period between the 12th and 16th centuries, and are tradi-
tionally considered to have been set up by monks of the great moorland
abbeys to mark safe routes across the moor. GUIDE STONES were set up from
the late 17th century to mark routes for pack horses and 'jobbers' between
towns. MILESTONES came into their own with the creation of turnpike
roads, and most date from the latter part of the 19th century.

BOUNDARY STONES

From prehistoric times, people and communities have established territories,
and set up markers in the landscape to define them. Some Bronze Age burial
mounds may have served this function. Natural features have been used,
prehistoric and medieval monuments reused, and new stones erected for the
purpose. They define ownership, manors, mines, military ranges, parishes,
and so on.

GLOSSARY
PREHISTORIC DARTMOOR

Chamber Tombs: Long (up to 48m) earthen mounds with a stone chamber at one end where multiple or successive burials took place. They were erected during the neolithic period (probably in the third millennium BC), in small clearances in the woodland cover. Not more than a dozen examples are known on Dartmoor, all on the fringes of the present day moorland; most have lost much, if not all of their earthen mounds. Spinsters' Rock (illustrated), of which only the chamber remains, fell down and was re-erected in the 1860s.

chamber tomb

Round Cairns: Round mounds, principally of stone, perhaps dating from the third millennium to around the middle of the second millennium BC. These mounds covered burials which were contained within pits or a cist (see over). Round cairns succeeded the chamber tombs and, although some may have covered more than one individual internment, many (the smaller examples) did not. Cairns vary in size from 3 to 4m in diameter, and less than 1m in height, to well over 20m and sometimes as much as 40m in diameter and 3.5 m in height. The smaller cairns are believed to be generally earlier in date and often have a vegetation cover different from the surrounding area. The larger cairns

round cairn

that were sited on prominent ridges and hilltops may well have also served as territorial boundary markers.

Cists: These are 'boxes', measuring 1m x 0.5m on average, formed of granite slabs, usually sunk into the ground to a depth of about 0.5m. They contained single burials – crouched inhumations or, perhaps more commonly, cremations, and were covered by small round cairns. In the bottom of some cists, pits containing charcoal have been found. They belong to the earlier part of the second

millennium BC. Most, if not all, of the known Dartmoor cists were excavated in the 19th or earlier 20th century; in some were found sherds of beaker-shaped pots, flint arrowheads and other artefacts.

Cairn Circles: Here, a single burial (often within a cist), was covered by a low round cairn. The limits of the cairn are marked by a circle of upright granite slabs, not touching each other, often leaning outwards.

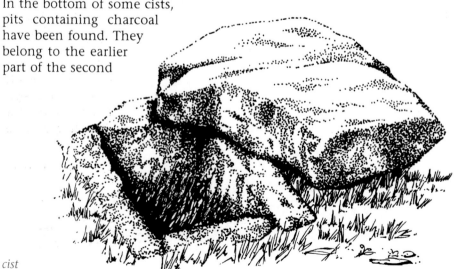

cist

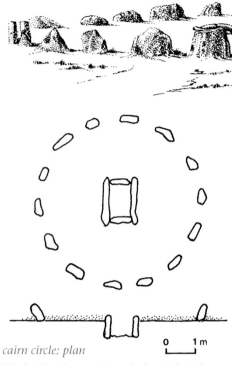

cairn circle

examples are known on Dartmoor, but of course this type of monument can only be recognised where the stones protrude from the cairn material. Most are sited close to or in a direct relationship to stone rows.

Ring Cairns: (See over) A level or slightly hollowed area is surrounded by a low circular or oval stone bank. Excavated examples of this type of

cairn circle: plan

Kerb Circles: A single burial (often within a cist), covered by a shallow spread of stone. The monument is bounded by a contiguous or a very close-set ring of low stones.

Multiple Stone Circles: (See over) Concentric rings of slab-like stones, within a low round cairn. Some ten

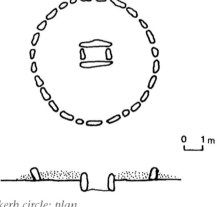

kerb circle: plan

kerb circle

31

multiple stone circle

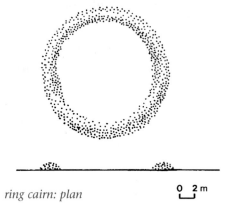

multiple stone circle: plan

`0 ___ 3 m`

Tor Cairns: The tors – in the main, granite outcrops – of Dartmoor are naturally dominant features. Some of these tors (or parts of them) were encircled by low banks of stone, or incorporated in a round cairn.

Cairnfields: A few groups of small cairns, numbering from 20 to 30, have been found in various parts of the moor, particularly in the north western quarter. The cairns are very

monument in Wales have proved to contain burials. Within the only two examples on Dartmoor to have been investigated were pits containing charcoal, but no evidence for burial was discovered; they were found to have been constructed around 1600–1800 BC.

ring cairn: plan

`0 __ 2 m`

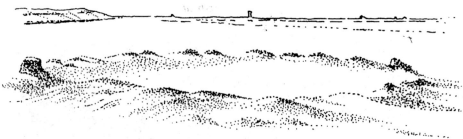

ring cairn

32

stone row

low, often only distinguishable because they have a different vegetation cover from the surrounding area. They are thought to date back to the earlier part of the second millennium BC. Not all necessarily covered burials; some may be clearance cairns.

Clearance Cairns: These are indistinguishable from the round cairns, being a mound of small stones, removed from an area to be cultivated or converted to pasture.

Clearance cairns can also date from medieval and later periods!

Stone Rows: Alignments of upright stones, which may be anything from 32m to 3.4 kilometres long and from 2.5m to less than 10cm high. More than 60 stone rows survive on Dartmoor; nearly half this number are single rows; almost the same number are formed of parallel lines and are called double stone rows. Only five examples of triple or multiple stone rows are known.

stone row

33

menhir

Menhirs: These are tall, upright stones (the tallest reaching 4.2m), which sometimes occur at the end of stone rows, but can also be found in isolation.

Stone Circles: Free-standing circles of upright stones, lacking any associated burial mound. The smaller examples are about 10–13m in diameter, the larger ones up to 33m. Limited investigation in the 19th century produced fragments of charcoal, but their purpose remains unclear. They were probably used for ceremonial purposes and/or perhaps as megalithic calendars.

Hut Circles: These are the remains of the round stone-walled structures, first built on Dartmoor during the second millennium BC, but continuing in this form into the first millennium BC. Four different construction methods of the stone walls have been observed: (i) a bank of rubble; (ii) single orthostats (usually of granite slabs) around the inner edge of the hut circle, with an external rubble bank; (iii) concentric rings of orthostatic walls with earth and rubble filling; and (iv) coursed drystone.

Almost three quarters of the Dartmoor stone rows have a burial monument at one end; a number have a tall terminal stone (or MENHIR). Some stone rows terminate in a blocking stone – a stone set sideways across the end of a row.

In a few areas on Dartmoor, two or more stone rows can be found together in a ritual complex, often in association with other monuments such as stone circles and cairns.

stone circle

*reconstruction drawing
of a hut circle*

Hut circles vary in size from 3–10m in diameter. Excavation suggests that the roof structure in many cases consisted of a ring of wooden posts within the hut circle; to these were probably fixed just above head height, a ring beam upon which rested the main roof timbers. The roof was conical, and probably covered with straw, heather or turf. Some hut circles contain hearths, suggesting that they were dwellings, but others may have been used for storage or as workshops.

Enclosures (or Pounds): Some hut circle settlements of the second millennium BC are surrounded by enclosure walls. In some cases, these walls were built to keep animals away from the dwellings; in others, they may have formed a safe area for people and stock. In one instance, it has been demonstrated by excavation that the enclosure wall was built some time after the construction of the first hut circle on the site.

Reaves: (See over) These are the land boundaries established by the Dartmoor communities during the middle of the second millennium BC. Excavation has shown that some reaves at least were of two phases. The first involved the creation of a low hedgebank of soil and turf; in the

a prehistoric enclosure

second phase the banks were capped with stone. Remains of gateways in the reaves have been found. Four main types of reave have been identified:

(i) *Terminal Reaves* – These are the boundaries which, cutting across the hillslopes of Dartmoor, defined the limits of enclosed land during the

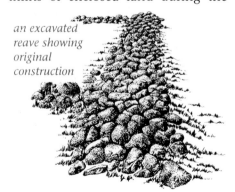

an excavated reave showing original construction

middle of the second millennium BC.

(ii) *Parallel Reaves* – Within the areas defined by the terminal reaves, land was further divided by the construction of parallel land boundaries, set at right angles to the terminal reave, and thus aligned up and down the hill and valley slopes. These created long, narrow, rectangular fields which, we assume, facilitated the controlled movement of stock.

(iii) *Cross Reaves* – Within the parallel reave systems, smaller fields were created by the construction of boundaries cutting across the areas between the parallel reaves.

(iv) *Contour Reaves* – These land boundaries snake across the contours, particularly on the southern

36

and western sides of Dartmoor, above the main areas of prehistoric enclosures. They are often incomplete, but seem to mark a division between grazing zones.

Hillforts: Defended settlements (containing hut circles) of the middle and later Iron Age, sited on hilltops on the moorland fringe, and demarcated by deep ditches and high ramparts. They may express an increasingly aggressive lifestyle at this time. Three hillforts overlooking the valley of the River Teign on north-east Dartmoor are sited very close together, and suggest an atmosphere of tension. One of these, Wooston, has a complicated arrangement of outworks (embanked enclosures) which may have been constructed to provide a safe haven for stock.

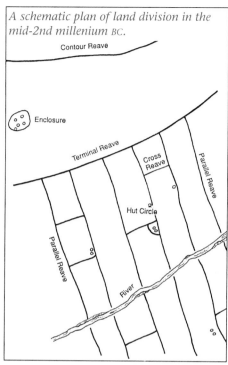

A schematic plan of land division in the mid-2nd millenium BC.

Frances Griffith - Devon County Council

Cranbrook hillfort

37

MEDIEVAL DARTMOOR

Post-Roman Memorial Stones: 5th–7th centuries AD: About a dozen examples of these have been found on the Dartmoor fringes, none in its original position. They commemorate tribal leaders, some of whom were of the (new) Christian faith. The script is either in Latin and/or Ogham – horizontal and vertical lines incised on the edges of the stones.

Post-Roman memorial stone

Longhouses: The typical medieval Dartmoor farmhouse. A single-storey rectangular building built into the slope and divided by opposing doors in the long sides. The animals (chiefly cattle) were sheltered in the lower end, down which ran a central drain. The humans occupied the upper end; food and heat was provided by a central open hearth. In the longhouses of the 12th–14th centuries, there was no physical division between the animal and human parts, and the animals would have been tethered. The longhouse continued to be built on Dartmoor until the 18th century, by which time it had become a sophisticated building with a separate entrance for the cattle; it was of two storeys and had a fireplace. The longhouses which are still lived in are no earlier than 15th or 16th century in date.

Corn-drying Barns: (See p.40) During the 14th century, the climate worsened and it was no longer possible for crops to ripen naturally in the field. Cereals were dried in kilns and ovens to provide seed and milling corn.

Infields and Outfields: Infield-outfield cultivation is typical of

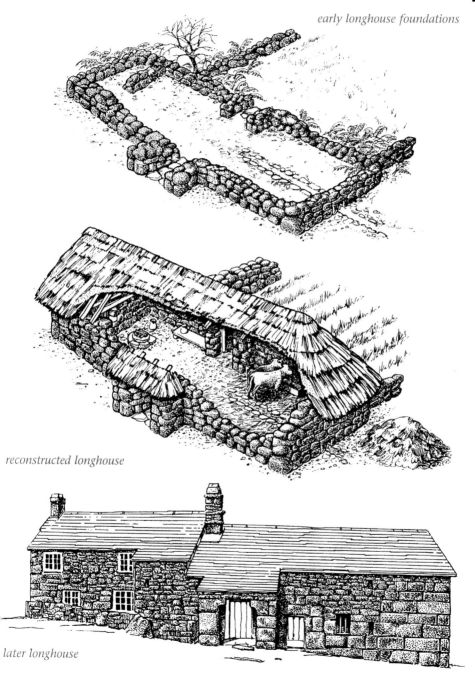

early longhouse foundations

reconstructed longhouse

later longhouse

corn-drying barn

upland areas, where there was plentiful pasture. Large fields (infields), bounded by hedgebanks, were created nearest to the medieval farmsteads; these were subdivided into strips, sometimes defined by balks (unploughed ridges), where cereal crops were grown. Within the infields, a small community of farmers would divide the land between themselves by each cultivating a number of scattered strips interspersed with those of his neighbours. Outfields were won from the open moor; they were used primarily for pasture, but, when market forces were dictated, were occasionally taken into cultivation.

Corn Ditches: The corn ditch, which divided enclosed lands from areas of open grazing, has an asymmetrical profile: a ditch and vertical stone wall face against the common or grazing land and deterred grazing livestock from entering the farmland; the sloping bank behind allowed animals that had managed

corn ditch

to breach the boundary to leave with comparative ease. The origins of the corn ditch go back to the time when central Dartmoor was used as a royal hunting ground; the wild deer could be thus contained within the open moor. Parallel or concentric arrangements of corn ditches can often illustrate the fluctuations of enclosure during medieval times.

Strip Lynchets: Lynchets are formed by the build-up of soil

40

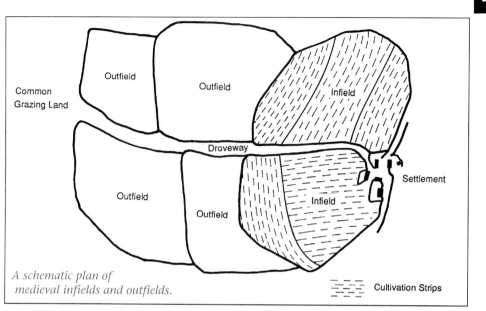

A schematic plan of
medieval infields and outfields.

Labels in figure: Common Grazing Land, Outfield, Outfield, Infield, Droveway, Outfield, Outfield, Infield, Settlement, Cultivation Strips

behind a linear barrier, often formed of stones cleared from the area of cultivation. The narrow terraces so created on the Dartmoor hillslopes provided a much needed depth of soil, and facilitated drainage. Sometimes strip lynchets were asso-ciated with a single farmstead but, more commonly, were shared between the inhabitants of a hamlet.

Ridge and Furrow: (See over) The formation of parallel ridges of soil,

strip lynchets

Stephen Woods

ridge and furrow

separated by furrows, created deeper and better-draining soils. The narrower type of ridge and furrow (illustrated), is thought to date from the 16-18th centuries and was created either by ploughing or hand digging. It represents a form of outfield cultivation. Broader ridges may be medieval in date.

Enclosed Strips: The enclosure of individual strips of land, which had formerly been unenclosed and lay within communally worked large areas, began in the late medieval period. In the photograph the enclosing hedgebanks follow the sinuous shape of the earlier strips.

Pillow Mounds: Elongated artificial rabbit buries are known as pillow mounds because of their shape. In essence they provided a dry and easily dug home for the rabbit, which

enclosed strips

could then be trapped with ferrets or dogs and nets.

Vermin Traps: Weasels and stoats – the main predators of the rabbit – were caught in traps which first

pillow mound

42

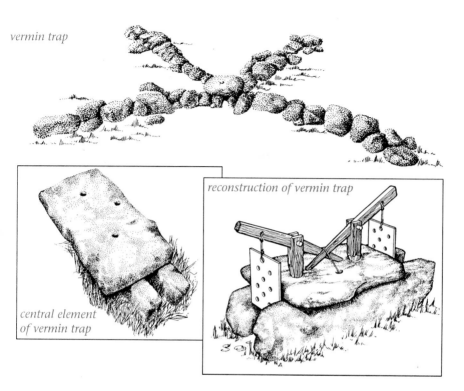

vermin trap

reconstruction of vermin trap

central element of vermin trap

unnelled them into a small granite
unnel (usually 1m x 0.5m), and
hen secured them there with slate
hutters, triggered to drop when the
nimal entered the trap.

urgage Plots: (See over) Towns of
he medieval period exhibit some
lement of planning. Houses – or
hops – were sited along the street
rontage, and behind these extended
ong narrow plots occupied by work-
hops, horticultural gardens and
ields.

astles: (See over) The medieval
astles on Dartmoor were built
either at the time of the Norman
Conquest (c.1087–88 in Devon) or
during the civil wars between
Stephen and Matilda in the mid-
12th century. Some (eg Hembury,
Buckfastleigh) originally had structures built in timber, so that now
only the earthworks survive. Others
(Okehampton, illustrated), had
stone buildings from the earliest
times. There are two basic forms of
medieval castle. The first is the
motte and bailey. The motte was an
artificial mound upon which was
built the stronghold, or keep, and
the bailey was a defended area
containing the domestic buildings.

43

burgage plots

The second is the ringwork, where a roughly circular area was enclosed by a rampart. The stone 'castle' at Lydford was first built as a free standing tower serving as a court-house and gaol for the tin industry. It was later remodelled so that it took on the appearance of a motte and bailey castle.

Churches: Most of Dartmoor's churches were enlarged or refurbished during the 15th and 16th centuries. We can detect regional

motte and bailey castle

influences at work – tall slim towers at Widecombe-in-the-Moor (illustrated, below) and other churches on the eastern side of the Moor, short stumpy towers with crocketed pinnacles (eg at Lydford, above) to the west.

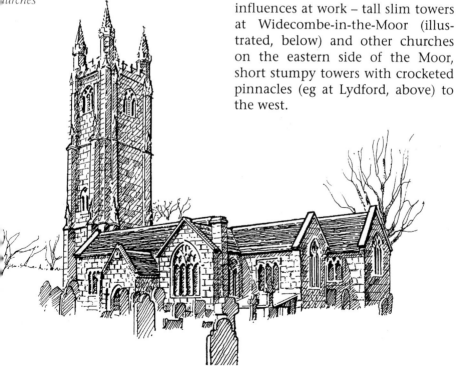

INDUSTRIAL DARTMOOR

Stream-working: Alluvial deposits of tin ore were extracted from the valley bottoms using the power of the river or stream to wash away lighter waste material. The waste material was formed into spoil heaps which were used to divert the water on to fresh deposits of tin ore. These are often to be seen in parallel sinuous lines, and are sometimes revetted by dry-stone walling.

Trial Pits: Prospecting pits, rectangular in shape, excavated at right-angles to the expected line of a tin lode; a crescent-shaped bank of spoil can often be found on the down-slope side of the pit.

Lode-back Pits: Tin lodes below the ground surface were extracted by the excavation of a series of pits, up to 3m deep, each surrounded by its own spoil heap. The pits are usually sited close together following the line of the lode.

stream-working

openworks

Openworks: Linear, V-shaped gullies, some as much as 200m long and 10m deep, following the east–west direction of the tin-bearing lodes. In the bottom of some can be found shallow shafts or lode-back pits. Some openworks have leats (artificial water channels) asso-ciated with them; water was used perhaps with heat to split the rock, or to wash away waste material.

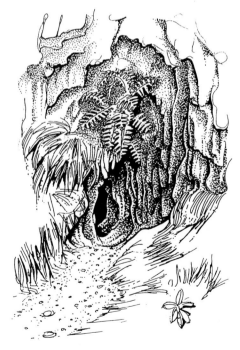

Shaft-mining: Circular, vertical pits up to 10m wide, usually surrounded by a ring of spoil which resembles a pudding basin. Most surviving examples belong to the 19th century, although shaft-mining on Dartmoor began in the 16th century.

Adits: Horizontal tunnels cut into hillsides for draining water from shafts or to provide access.

adit

47

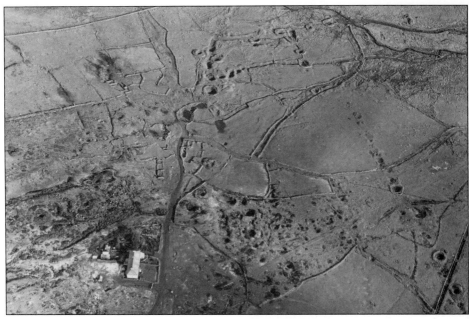

shaft mining

Tin Mills: (15th–18th centuries) These are usually small (up to 10 x 5m) stone buildings, within which tin ore was either crushed or smelted, or sometimes both. These operations were powered by water, and the tin mills have a wheelpit to one side. Within the mills can often be seen mortar stones, furnaces and/or mouldstones.

tin mill

reconstruction of a tin mill showing
stamps, furnace and mouldstone

leat

Leats: Artificial water channels, bringing water to an industrial site, such as a tin mill, or to a farmstead or settlement. The leat which served the mines at Vitifer was 7 miles (11km) long. Drake's Leat, constructed in 1590–91 to provide water to the town of Plymouth, is 17 miles (27km) long.

stamps

Mortar stones: Mortar stones, slabs of granite upon which tin ore was crushed in a tin mill, are easily recognisable by the cup-shaped hollows worn in their surface by the pounding of the stamps. Most stones have two hollows side by side left by a pair of stamps, but there are examples of triple mortar stones. Sometimes, when a mortar stone became too worn, it was turned over and used again.

Stamps: Stamps were used to crush tin ore. Wooden poles, with iron shoes, were driven in a trip action by a waterwheel, and descended vertically on to the ore. Their presence in tin mills of 15th–18th century date, is indicated by the existence of mortar stones (see above). A few rare photographs of 19th-century stamps survive from one of which this illustration is taken.

Dressing Floors: Pits, often rectangular structures with stone-walled sides, where water was used to clean the crushed tin ore and separate the tin concentrate from waste. They can appear as very shallow depressions in the ground.

Buddles: Most surviving buddles on Dartmoor belong to the 19th century, by which time the earlier rectangular shape had largely been replaced by a circular one. In the round buddle (illustrated) – which has an average diameter of 3 to 4.8m – a mixture of crushed tin ore and water was agitated by revolving overhead sweeps; the heavier material (ie that containing the most metal) settled nearest the centre.

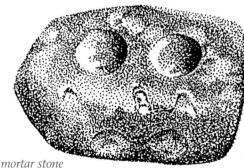

mortar stone

a buddle

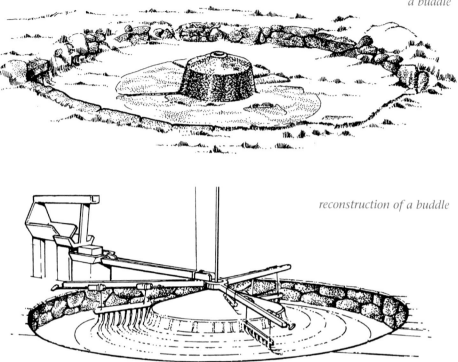

reconstruction of a buddle

Furnaces: In a number of tin mills, remains of blast furnaces can be seen, resembling substantial, narrow fireplaces. The heat of the furnaces was enhanced by the use of giant bellows, which were powered by the waterwheel.

Mouldstone: After smelting, molten tin was poured into a mould carved out of a block of granite. The average ingot in the period between the 15th and 17th centuries weighed 883kg (195 lbs).

Charcoal Burners' Hearths: (See over) Charcoal was an important source of fuel on Dartmoor, vital to its industries. The trees in the wooded valleys were coppiced; their branches were cut, stacked on to a platform, and covered with turf and earth to reduce the amount of oxygen. The stack was then burnt slowly, often for several days. The

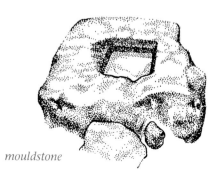

mouldstone

charcoal burners' hearth

platforms, or hearths, are circular or elliptical in form averaging 2–4m in diameter.

Wheelpits: Water was the main source of power on Dartmoor for many centuries. It was used to drive machinery for a wide range of purposes, for example in the manufacture of tin, gunpowder, and for threshing straw or grinding corn. According to the lie of the land, or the purpose to which they were put, these rectangular stone-walled pits were either sunk wholly or partially into the ground or attached to a building. Water was brought to them via a leat and sometimes an elevated wooden channel, or launder. The largest wheelpit on Dartmoor contained a wheel 70ft (21.3m) in diameter.

Beehive Huts: Small stone-built stores or shelters, whose shape resembles that of an old-fashioned beehive. Most examples are now ruinous and have lost their tapering roofs.

wheelpit and reconstruction of waterwheel

beehive hut

dry

engine house

silver-lead industries; all but one are in a very ruinous condition.

Wedge and Groove: Before 1800, surface granite was split by this method. A line of narrow grooves was cut into the rock using a sledge-hammer and a narrow chisel-like object. Wooden wedges (sometimes soaked to make them expand) were

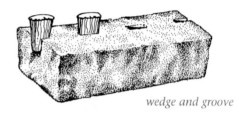

wedge and groove

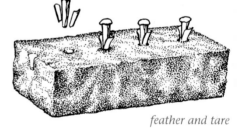

feather and tare

Drys: These buildings were heated by a boiler and used to dry the clothes (and also presumably the bodies!) of underground workers in the mines. The tall chimney was sited at the end of a long flue, which provided heating. In some cases a smithy was also housed in the same building.

Engine Houses: Engine houses were constructed to house steam engines used to pump water from nearby mine-shafts. Most of the few Dartmoor examples date from the latter part of the 19th century, and are associated with the copper and

hammered into the grooves, thus forcing the stone to split along the line of the grooves.

Feather and Tare: This method of splitting surface granite dates from about 1800. A line of circular holes was driven into the stone using an iron bar known as a 'jumper'. Into the holes were set metal wedges (tares), supported on either side by pairs of concave metal pieces

gateposts

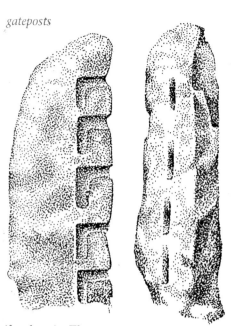

trough

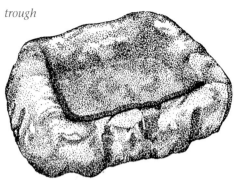

farmstead. Many were used to collect water from pumps or springs; others formed food receptacles for farm animals.

Crushers and Presses: Apples, cheese and furze (or gorse, which provided winter feed for stock) were all processed using granite artefacts. Redundant examples survive on some farms and abandoned examples exist on the moor.

(feathers). The tares were hit by a hammer until the stone split along the line of holes.

Gateposts: Before the advent of the hinged gate, gateways were closed by a series of wooden planks or bars, resting in slots carved into the stone post.

Troughs: Granite troughs were once a ubiquitous feature of the Dartmoor

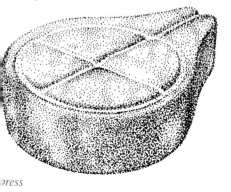

press

Millstones: (See over) The rough surface of granite provided ideal material to create millstones, which were used for a variety of purposes – milling corn, grinding tin and in the refining process of the basic ingredients of gunpowder. Sometimes, these were manufactured on the moor, and examples of abandoned work can still be seen.

Sett-Makers' Bankers: (See over) Often much of the preparation and dressing of the stone took place on site so as to save unnecessary labour and the cost of transporting heavy stone. Sett-makers' bankers (crude

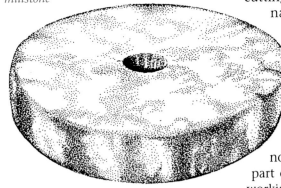
millstone

cuttings can be recognised by narrow, parallel depressions (called 'peat ties') in the surface of the ground.

stone benches) were used by masons in the preparation of paving stones, kerbs and setts.

Peat Cuttings: Peat first began to form on Dartmoor during the mesolithic period (c.8000 BC), and its growth accelerated in the second millennium BC. The peat deposits of Dartmoor today are a rich source for those who wish to understand the past environment of the area, as they contain pollen from plants growing here many thousands of years ago. Nevertheless, in the past peat was used by the inhabitants of Dartmoor as a source of fuel – domestic and industrial. Peat

China Clay: China clay is a derivative of granite, and has been used chiefly for what are known as 'sanitary wares'. Although the modern industry now dominates the south western part of the moor, at the abandoned workings of the 19th century can be seen the spoil heaps left during extraction of the resource and, at some distance, the remains of settling tanks (where the pure clay was separated out by flotation in water brought to site by an intricate systems of channels) and drying sheds.

Tramways: Here can be seen the precursor to the railway. A 'train' of trucks, bearing quarried granite was borne along a road created by L-shaped granite setts, and pulled by horses.

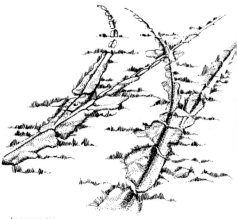

sett-makers' banker

tramway

BOUNDARIES AND BYWAYS

clapper bridge

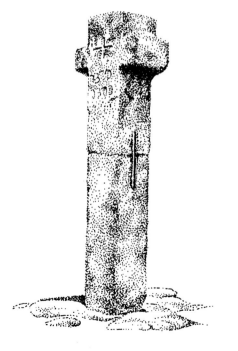

Clapper Bridges: The clapper bridge is one of Dartmoor's well-known features. Large granite slabs (or 'clappers') were laid across streams or rivers; either from bank to bank or resting upon piers in mid-stream. The word clapper is said to derive from the Anglo-Saxon word *cleaca* meaning 'bridging the stepping stones'.

Crosses: Granite crosses are characteristic of the Dartmoor landscape. A few were set up in villages or churchyards (perhaps as preaching crosses) but the majority were erected to waymark routes across the moor. Some have been lost, but originally the intention must have been that (the lie of the land and weather permitting) a traveller could see

cross

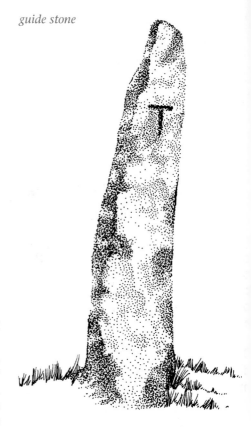

guide stone

from one cross to the next. Most have a cross-head with short arms; some also have crosses incised upon them. The majority of the Dartmoor crosses belong to the period between the 12th or 13th centuries and the middle of the 16th century, and are thought to have been set up by the monasteries (Buckland, Tavistock or Buckfast) located on the edge of the moorland.

Guide Stones: These marked routes between settlements, and were set up following an Act of Parliament in the late 17th century. The interesting feature about them is that, to modern eyes, they face the wrong way. Walking or riding from Ashburton to Tavistock, the traveller would encounter the inscribed letter 'A' rather than 'T', indicating the route behind, rather than that ahead.

Milestones: These either mark the distance between two or more places, or else the distance from one particular place or the progressive length of a routeway. Many roadside milestones are associated with the creation, in the late 18th century, of turnpikes – roads whose repair was the responsibility of a private trust who could levy tolls for their use. Some milestones described one distance in both miles and poles

...ilestone

centuries. Their inscriptions may record – often by initials – the name of the area or the owner (illustrated: the Duke of Somerset on Haytor Down) or in the case of bridges (illustrated), the area for which the county was responsible for maintenance.

County boundary stone

...nits of $5^{1}/_{2}$ yards, 5m). Other types milestone are associated with her features or events, for example e Haytor tramway, or the paroling French prisoners of war in the rly 19th century.

...undary Stones: Inscribed boundry stones are difficult to date, but any belong to the last two or three

...undary stone

59

FURTHER READING

Brewer, D. *A Field Guide to the Boundary Markers in and around Dartmoc* Devon Books, 1986.

Butler, J. *The Dartmoor Atlas of Antiquities*, (five volumes). Devon Book 1991-96.

Devon Archaeological Society *Devon Archaeology No 3: Dartmoor issu* Devon Archaeological Society, 1991.

Fleming, A. *The Dartmoor Reaves*. Batsford, 1988.

Fox, Aileen. *Prehistoric Hillforts in Devon*. Devon Books 1996.

Gill, C. (editor) *Dartmoor: A New Study*. David & Charles, 1983.

Greeves, T. *Tin Mines and Miners of Dartmoor*. Devon Books, 1988,1993.

Griffiths, D. (Ed). *The Archaeology of Dartmoor: Perspectives from the 1990* Proceedings of the Devon Archaeological Society No 52 (1994).

Harris, H. *The Industrial Archaeology of Dartmoor*. Peninsula Press, 1992.

Starkey, F.H. *Dartmoor Crosses and Some Ancient Tracks*. F.H. Starkey, 1983.

Weir, J. (editor) *Dartmoor National Park Guide*. Webb & Bower/Micha* Joseph, 1987.

Woods, S. *Dartmoor Stone*. Devon Books, 1988.

Worth, R.H. *Worth's Dartmoor*. David & Charles, 1971; Peninsula Press, 199*

INDEX

HELP PROTECT THE FUTURE OF OUR PAST
Please remember:

1. Dartmoor is one of the most important archaeological landscapes in Britain. Each individual feature may have a vital clue to the past.

2. Many archaeological sites are protected by law (the *Ancient Monuments and Archaeological Areas Act 1979*). YOU MAY BE BREAKING THE LAW if you disturb them.

3. Many archaeological features are smaller than you might expect. Some are only a few centimetres high.

4. If you are not sure whether something is an archaeological site or not, give it the benefit of the doubt and leave well alone.

5. Never disturb an archaeological site or ruined structure by moving stones around.

6. Never dig in or around an archaeological site. Information buried below ground is as important to the archaeologist as that which can be seen above ground.

7. Do not camp or light fires in or around archaeological sites.

8. Do not use archaeological sites to store equipment or as hiding places or as bivouac sites.

9. Mineshafts and old mine workings can be dangerous.

10. A pile of stones is not just a pile of stones. A moment's carelessness can destroy thousands of years of history.